A Note to Parents and Teachers

Kids can imagine, kids can laugh and kids can learn to read with this exciting new series of first readers. Each book in the Kids Can Read series has been especially written, illustrated and designed for beginning readers. Humorous, easy-to-read stories, appealing characters and topics, and engaging illustrations make for books that kids will want to read over and over again.

To make selecting a book easy for kids, parents and teachers, the Kids Can Read series offers three levels based on different reading abilities:

Level 1: Kids Can Start to Read

Short stories, simple sentences, easy vocabulary, lots of repetition and visual clues for kids just beginning to read.

Level 2: Kids Can Read with Help

Longer stories, varied sentences, increased vocabulary, some repetition and visual clues for kids who have some reading skills, but may need a little help.

Level 3: Kids Can Read Alone

More challenging topics, more complex sentences, advanced vocabulary, language play, minimal repetition and visual clues for kids who are reading by themselves.

With the Kids Can Read series, kids can enter a new and exciting world of reading!

Helen Keller

For Jessica Jorda—Let nothing stand in your way—E.M.
For my children and my grandson— A.K.

 ® Kids Can Read is a registered trademark of Kids Can Press Ltd.

Text © 2007 Elizabeth MacLeod
Illustrations © 2007 Andrej Krystoforski

Kids Can Press acknowledges the financial support of the Government of Ontario, through the Ontario Media Development Corporation's Ontario Book Initiative; the Ontario Arts Council; the Canada Council for the Arts; and the Government of Canada, through the BPIDP, for our publishing activity.

Published in Canada by
Kids Can Press Ltd.
29 Birch Avenue
Toronto, ON M4V 1E2

Published in the U.S. by
Kids Can Press Ltd.
2250 Military Road
Tonawanda, NY 14150

www.kidscanpress.com

Edited by David MacDonald
Designed by Marie Bartholomew
Printed and bound in Singapore

Educational consultant: Maureen Skinner Weiner, United Synagogue Day School, Willowdale, Ontario.
Bias reviewer: Margaret Hoogeveen

The hardcover edition of this book is smyth sewn casebound.
The paperback edition of this book is limp sewn with a drawn-on cover.

CM 07 0 9 8 7 6 5 4 3 2 1
CM PA 07 0 9 8 7 6 5 4 3 2 1

Library and Archives Canada Cataloguing in Publication

MacLeod, Elizabeth
     Helen Keller / written by Elizabeth MacLeod;
illustrated by Andrej Krystoforski.

(Kids Can read)
ISBN 978-1-55337-999-7 (bound). ISBN 978-1-55453-000-7 (pbk.)

1. Keller, Helen, 1880–1968—Juvenile literature. 2. Sullivan, Annie, 1866-1936—Juvenile literature. 3. Deafblind women—United States—Biography—Juvenile literature. I. Krystoforski, Andrej, 1943–
II. Title. III. Series: Kids Can read (Toronto, Ont.)

HV1624.K4M33 2007   j362.4'1092   C2006-906848-8

Kids Can Press is a **l'orus**™ Entertainment company

Helen Keller

Written by Elizabeth MacLeod
Illustrated by Andrej Krystoforski

Kids Can Press

Close your eyes tightly. Put your hands over your ears so you cannot hear a thing. Now, imagine living in such a dark, silent world. This was the world of Helen Keller.

Helen could not see or hear, but she wrote books and traveled around the world. She even went to college.

Helen showed everyone that people who are deaf and blind can do many things.

Helen was born in 1880 in Alabama, in the United States. She was a smart, happy baby who could see and hear.

But when Helen was 19 months old, she became very sick. She had a high fever. Her mother and father did all they could to keep Helen alive.

Suddenly one day, Helen's fever was gone. Her parents were happy — at first. But then they realized the fever had made Helen deaf and blind.

Her parents were worried. What would life be like for their daughter?

Life was very difficult for Helen. Most young children learn to speak by listening to people. But Helen could not hear, so she did not learn to speak.

Helen could not tell her parents what she wanted. Sometimes she kicked and screamed with anger. She broke lamps and dishes.

But Helen was smart. She made up signs for things. If she wanted some nice, cold ice cream, she shivered. Her father wore glasses, so Helen's sign for him was pretending to put on glasses.

The Kellers hoped to find someone who could help Helen. Sometimes they visited doctors who lived far away. But no one could do anything for their little girl.

Finally, one doctor told the Kellers to visit Alexander Graham Bell.

You may know that Alexander Graham Bell invented the telephone. But he was also famous for teaching deaf children how to speak.

Helen and her father went to visit Alexander. When he saw Helen, Alexander got an idea. He handed her his watch.

Alexander knew Helen could not see the watch or hear it tick. But he thought she would like to feel the watch ticking.

Helen loved the watch — and Alexander. They were friends for the rest of their lives.

Alexander told the Kellers to visit a special school for blind people in Boston, Massachusetts. There they found a teacher for Helen.

In March 1887, Annie Sullivan arrived at the Kellers' home to teach Helen.

Annie knew sign language. Sign language is a way that many deaf people talk to each other by making shapes with their hands. Annie wanted to teach Helen to talk using sign language.

Right away, Annie began using sign language to spell words into Helen's hand. Helen could feel the shapes Annie made.

Helen repeated the finger-spellings back to Annie. But Helen did not know that they stood for letters. How could Annie make Helen understand?

One morning in early April, Annie had an idea. She hurried Helen over to a water pump. Annie pumped cold water over Helen's hands. As the water gushed out, Annie spelled "W-A-T-E-R" into Helen's hand.

Suddenly, Helen became completely still. Annie could tell that Helen finally understood! Right away, Helen began asking the name of everything she touched.

By the end of the day, Helen had learned to finger-spell 30 words. Soon, she was spelling out sentences.

In just six months, Helen learned 625 words. Annie also taught Helen how to read using Braille. Braille is a kind of writing that uses a pattern of dots pressed into paper for each letter of the alphabet. You can feel the dots with your fingertips.

Helen also learned a way to know what people were saying. She put her fingers right on their lips. Helen could tell what words they were saying by the way their lips moved.

When Helen was 16, she decided that one day she wanted to go to college. But first she would have to pass tests. It would be hard work, but she was used to that!

Helen passed the tests and started going to college when she was 20. Annie went to school with Helen.

Annie listened to what each teacher said and spelled the words into Helen's hands. After class, Helen rushed to write down what she remembered.

Do you say facts out loud to help remember them? When Helen studied, she finger-spelled to herself!

At college, Helen did not spend all her time doing schoolwork. She also hiked, rode horses and swam.

Helen became the first deaf-blind person in the United States to finish college. She had some of the best marks in her class!

Now Helen had to decide what she wanted to do next.

Helen decided to give talks about her life. But it was hard for her to speak clearly because she could not hear the words she was saying.

Helen and Annie came up with a plan. Helen would say something and then Annie would repeat it so people could understand.

When Helen finished her first talk, she was sure she had not done well. Then she felt the floor shaking because everyone was clapping so loudly. Helen could tell the crowd thought she was wonderful!

A few years later, Helen became part
of a show. The show had lots of dancers,
actors and even clowns.

With Annie helping, Helen talked
about her life and answered questions.
The shows were hard work. But Helen
loved doing them — and audiences
loved her!

Later on, Helen traveled around the world giving talks. At that time, most people believed that there were many things a blind person could not do. Helen changed people's ideas about blind people.

As she traveled, Helen collected millions of dollars to help people who could not see.

Helen died in 1968. She was 87 years old. At her funeral, someone used sign language to repeat every word. That way, all of Helen's deaf friends could understand.

People still remember the many amazing
things Helen did.

More facts about Helen

• Helen was born on June 27, 1880. She died on June 1, 1968.

• June 27 is Helen Keller Day. People all around the world celebrate her life on that day.

• Dogs were Helen's favorite animal. She always owned one or two.